This Blood ⌒ ⌒ ⌒
belongs to:

Name:	
Address:	
Email:	
Phone:	

Emergency Contacts:

SUNDAY   DATE:

MEALS	READINGS	BEFORE	AFTER	NOTES
	BREAKFAST			
	LUNCH			
	DINNER			
	SNACKS			
	BEDTIME			

MONDAY   DATE:

MEALS	READINGS	BEFORE	AFTER	NOTES
	BREAKFAST			
	LUNCH			
	DINNER			
	SNACKS			
	BEDTIME			

TUESDAY   DATE:

MEALS	READINGS	BEFORE	AFTER	NOTES
	BREAKFAST			
	LUNCH			
	DINNER			
	SNACKS			
	BEDTIME			

WEDNESDAY   DATE:

MEALS	READINGS	BEFORE	AFTER	NOTES
	BREAKFAST			
	LUNCH			
	DINNER			
	SNACKS			
	BEDTIME			

THURSDAY	DATE:			
MEALS	**READINGS**	**BEFORE**	**AFTER**	**NOTES**
	BREAKFAST			
	LUNCH			
	DINNER			
	SNACKS			
	BEDTIME			

FRIDAY	DATE:			
MEALS	**READINGS**	**BEFORE**	**AFTER**	**NOTES**
	BREAKFAST			
	LUNCH			
	DINNER			
	SNACKS			
	BEDTIME			

SATURDAY	DATE:			
MEALS	**READINGS**	**BEFORE**	**AFTER**	**NOTES**
	BREAKFAST			
	LUNCH			
	DINNER			
	SNACKS			
	BEDTIME			

NOTES

_____

_____

_____

_____

SUNDAY   DATE:

MEALS	READINGS	BEFORE	AFTER	NOTES
	BREAKFAST			
	LUNCH			
	DINNER			
	SNACKS			
	BEDTIME			

MONDAY   DATE:

MEALS	READINGS	BEFORE	AFTER	NOTES
	BREAKFAST			
	LUNCH			
	DINNER			
	SNACKS			
	BEDTIME			

TUESDAY   DATE:

MEALS	READINGS	BEFORE	AFTER	NOTES
	BREAKFAST			
	LUNCH			
	DINNER			
	SNACKS			
	BEDTIME			

WEDNESDAY   DATE:

MEALS	READINGS	BEFORE	AFTER	NOTES
	BREAKFAST			
	LUNCH			
	DINNER			
	SNACKS			
	BEDTIME			

THURSDAY	DATE:			
MEALS	**READINGS**	**BEFORE**	**AFTER**	**NOTES**
	BREAKFAST			
	LUNCH			
	DINNER			
	SNACKS			
	BEDTIME			

FRIDAY	DATE:			
MEALS	**READINGS**	**BEFORE**	**AFTER**	**NOTES**
	BREAKFAST			
	LUNCH			
	DINNER			
	SNACKS			
	BEDTIME			

SATURDAY	DATE:			
MEALS	**READINGS**	**BEFORE**	**AFTER**	**NOTES**
	BREAKFAST			
	LUNCH			
	DINNER			
	SNACKS			
	BEDTIME			

NOTES

_____

_____

_____

_____

SUNDAY　　DATE:

MEALS	READINGS	BEFORE	AFTER	NOTES
	BREAKFAST			
	LUNCH			
	DINNER			
	SNACKS			
	BEDTIME			

MONDAY　　DATE:

MEALS	READINGS	BEFORE	AFTER	NOTES
	BREAKFAST			
	LUNCH			
	DINNER			
	SNACKS			
	BEDTIME			

TUESDAY　　DATE:

MEALS	READINGS	BEFORE	AFTER	NOTES
	BREAKFAST			
	LUNCH			
	DINNER			
	SNACKS			
	BEDTIME			

WEDNESDAY　　DATE:

MEALS	READINGS	BEFORE	AFTER	NOTES
	BREAKFAST			
	LUNCH			
	DINNER			
	SNACKS			
	BEDTIME			

THURSDAY		DATE:		
MEALS	**READINGS**	**BEFORE**	**AFTER**	**NOTES**
	BREAKFAST			
	LUNCH			
	DINNER			
	SNACKS			
	BEDTIME			

FRIDAY		DATE:		
MEALS	**READINGS**	**BEFORE**	**AFTER**	**NOTES**
	BREAKFAST			
	LUNCH			
	DINNER			
	SNACKS			
	BEDTIME			

SATURDAY		DATE:		
MEALS	**READINGS**	**BEFORE**	**AFTER**	**NOTES**
	BREAKFAST			
	LUNCH			
	DINNER			
	SNACKS			
	BEDTIME			

NOTES

_____

_____

_____

_____

SUNDAY DATE:

MEALS	READINGS	BEFORE	AFTER	NOTES
	BREAKFAST			
	LUNCH			
	DINNER			
	SNACKS			
	BEDTIME			

MONDAY DATE:

MEALS	READINGS	BEFORE	AFTER	NOTES
	BREAKFAST			
	LUNCH			
	DINNER			
	SNACKS			
	BEDTIME			

TUESDAY DATE:

MEALS	READINGS	BEFORE	AFTER	NOTES
	BREAKFAST			
	LUNCH			
	DINNER			
	SNACKS			
	BEDTIME			

WEDNESDAY DATE:

MEALS	READINGS	BEFORE	AFTER	NOTES
	BREAKFAST			
	LUNCH			
	DINNER			
	SNACKS			
	BEDTIME			

THURSDAY		DATE:		
MEALS	READINGS	BEFORE	AFTER	NOTES
	BREAKFAST			
	LUNCH			
	DINNER			
	SNACKS			
	BEDTIME			

FRIDAY		DATE:		
MEALS	READINGS	BEFORE	AFTER	NOTES
	BREAKFAST			
	LUNCH			
	DINNER			
	SNACKS			
	BEDTIME			

SATURDAY		DATE:		
MEALS	READINGS	BEFORE	AFTER	NOTES
	BREAKFAST			
	LUNCH			
	DINNER			
	SNACKS			
	BEDTIME			

NOTES

_____

_____

_____

_____

SUNDAY

DATE:

MEALS	READINGS	BEFORE	AFTER	NOTES
	BREAKFAST			
	LUNCH			
	DINNER			
	SNACKS			
	BEDTIME			

MONDAY

DATE:

MEALS	READINGS	BEFORE	AFTER	NOTES
	BREAKFAST			
	LUNCH			
	DINNER			
	SNACKS			
	BEDTIME			

TUESDAY

DATE:

MEALS	READINGS	BEFORE	AFTER	NOTES
	BREAKFAST			
	LUNCH			
	DINNER			
	SNACKS			
	BEDTIME			

WEDNESDAY

DATE:

MEALS	READINGS	BEFORE	AFTER	NOTES
	BREAKFAST			
	LUNCH			
	DINNER			
	SNACKS			
	BEDTIME			

THURSDAY   DATE:

MEALS	READINGS	BEFORE	AFTER	NOTES
	BREAKFAST			
	LUNCH			
	DINNER			
	SNACKS			
	BEDTIME			

FRIDAY   DATE:

MEALS	READINGS	BEFORE	AFTER	NOTES
	BREAKFAST			
	LUNCH			
	DINNER			
	SNACKS			
	BEDTIME			

SATURDAY   DATE:

MEALS	READINGS	BEFORE	AFTER	NOTES
	BREAKFAST			
	LUNCH			
	DINNER			
	SNACKS			
	BEDTIME			

NOTES

_____

_____

_____

_____

SUNDAY   DATE:

MEALS	READINGS	BEFORE	AFTER	NOTES
	BREAKFAST			
	LUNCH			
	DINNER			
	SNACKS			
	BEDTIME			

MONDAY   DATE:

MEALS	READINGS	BEFORE	AFTER	NOTES
	BREAKFAST			
	LUNCH			
	DINNER			
	SNACKS			
	BEDTIME			

TUESDAY   DATE:

MEALS	READINGS	BEFORE	AFTER	NOTES
	BREAKFAST			
	LUNCH			
	DINNER			
	SNACKS			
	BEDTIME			

WEDNESDAY   DATE:

MEALS	READINGS	BEFORE	AFTER	NOTES
	BREAKFAST			
	LUNCH			
	DINNER			
	SNACKS			
	BEDTIME			

THURSDAY   DATE:

MEALS	READINGS	BEFORE	AFTER	NOTES
	BREAKFAST			
	LUNCH			
	DINNER			
	SNACKS			
	BEDTIME			

FRIDAY   DATE:

MEALS	READINGS	BEFORE	AFTER	NOTES
	BREAKFAST			
	LUNCH			
	DINNER			
	SNACKS			
	BEDTIME			

SATURDAY   DATE:

MEALS	READINGS	BEFORE	AFTER	NOTES
	BREAKFAST			
	LUNCH			
	DINNER			
	SNACKS			
	BEDTIME			

NOTES

_____

_____

_____

_____

SUNDAY   DATE:

MEALS	READINGS	BEFORE	AFTER	NOTES
	BREAKFAST			
	LUNCH			
	DINNER			
	SNACKS			
	BEDTIME			

MONDAY   DATE:

MEALS	READINGS	BEFORE	AFTER	NOTES
	BREAKFAST			
	LUNCH			
	DINNER			
	SNACKS			
	BEDTIME			

TUESDAY   DATE:

MEALS	READINGS	BEFORE	AFTER	NOTES
	BREAKFAST			
	LUNCH			
	DINNER			
	SNACKS			
	BEDTIME			

WEDNESDAY   DATE:

MEALS	READINGS	BEFORE	AFTER	NOTES
	BREAKFAST			
	LUNCH			
	DINNER			
	SNACKS			
	BEDTIME			

THURSDAY		DATE:		
MEALS	**READINGS**	**BEFORE**	**AFTER**	**NOTES**
	BREAKFAST			
	LUNCH			
	DINNER			
	SNACKS			
	BEDTIME			

FRIDAY		DATE:		
MEALS	**READINGS**	**BEFORE**	**AFTER**	**NOTES**
	BREAKFAST			
	LUNCH			
	DINNER			
	SNACKS			
	BEDTIME			

SATURDAY		DATE:		
MEALS	**READINGS**	**BEFORE**	**AFTER**	**NOTES**
	BREAKFAST			
	LUNCH			
	DINNER			
	SNACKS			
	BEDTIME			

NOTES

SUNDAY DATE:

MEALS	READINGS	BEFORE	AFTER	NOTES
	BREAKFAST			
	LUNCH			
	DINNER			
	SNACKS			
	BEDTIME			

MONDAY DATE:

MEALS	READINGS	BEFORE	AFTER	NOTES
	BREAKFAST			
	LUNCH			
	DINNER			
	SNACKS			
	BEDTIME			

TUESDAY DATE:

MEALS	READINGS	BEFORE	AFTER	NOTES
	BREAKFAST			
	LUNCH			
	DINNER			
	SNACKS			
	BEDTIME			

WEDNESDAY DATE:

MEALS	READINGS	BEFORE	AFTER	NOTES
	BREAKFAST			
	LUNCH			
	DINNER			
	SNACKS			
	BEDTIME			

THURSDAY		DATE:		
MEALS	**READINGS**	**BEFORE**	**AFTER**	**NOTES**
	BREAKFAST			
	LUNCH			
	DINNER			
	SNACKS			
	BEDTIME			

FRIDAY		DATE:		
MEALS	**READINGS**	**BEFORE**	**AFTER**	**NOTES**
	BREAKFAST			
	LUNCH			
	DINNER			
	SNACKS			
	BEDTIME			

SATURDAY		DATE:		
MEALS	**READINGS**	**BEFORE**	**AFTER**	**NOTES**
	BREAKFAST			
	LUNCH			
	DINNER			
	SNACKS			
	BEDTIME			

NOTES

SUNDAY   DATE:

MEALS	READINGS	BEFORE	AFTER	NOTES
	BREAKFAST			
	LUNCH			
	DINNER			
	SNACKS			
	BEDTIME			

MONDAY   DATE:

MEALS	READINGS	BEFORE	AFTER	NOTES
	BREAKFAST			
	LUNCH			
	DINNER			
	SNACKS			
	BEDTIME			

TUESDAY   DATE:

MEALS	READINGS	BEFORE	AFTER	NOTES
	BREAKFAST			
	LUNCH			
	DINNER			
	SNACKS			
	BEDTIME			

WEDNESDAY   DATE:

MEALS	READINGS	BEFORE	AFTER	NOTES
	BREAKFAST			
	LUNCH			
	DINNER			
	SNACKS			
	BEDTIME			

THURSDAY	DATE:			
MEALS	READINGS	BEFORE	AFTER	NOTES
	BREAKFAST			
	LUNCH			
	DINNER			
	SNACKS			
	BEDTIME			

FRIDAY	DATE:			
MEALS	READINGS	BEFORE	AFTER	NOTES
	BREAKFAST			
	LUNCH			
	DINNER			
	SNACKS			
	BEDTIME			

SATURDAY	DATE:			
MEALS	READINGS	BEFORE	AFTER	NOTES
	BREAKFAST			
	LUNCH			
	DINNER			
	SNACKS			
	BEDTIME			

NOTES

SUNDAY   DATE:

MEALS	READINGS	BEFORE	AFTER	NOTES
	BREAKFAST			
	LUNCH			
	DINNER			
	SNACKS			
	BEDTIME			

MONDAY   DATE:

MEALS	READINGS	BEFORE	AFTER	NOTES
	BREAKFAST			
	LUNCH			
	DINNER			
	SNACKS			
	BEDTIME			

TUESDAY   DATE:

MEALS	READINGS	BEFORE	AFTER	NOTES
	BREAKFAST			
	LUNCH			
	DINNER			
	SNACKS			
	BEDTIME			

WEDNESDAY   DATE:

MEALS	READINGS	BEFORE	AFTER	NOTES
	BREAKFAST			
	LUNCH			
	DINNER			
	SNACKS			
	BEDTIME			

THURSDAY		DATE:		
MEALS	**READINGS**	**BEFORE**	**AFTER**	**NOTES**
	BREAKFAST			
	LUNCH			
	DINNER			
	SNACKS			
	BEDTIME			

FRIDAY		DATE:		
MEALS	**READINGS**	**BEFORE**	**AFTER**	**NOTES**
	BREAKFAST			
	LUNCH			
	DINNER			
	SNACKS			
	BEDTIME			

SATURDAY		DATE:		
MEALS	**READINGS**	**BEFORE**	**AFTER**	**NOTES**
	BREAKFAST			
	LUNCH			
	DINNER			
	SNACKS			
	BEDTIME			

NOTES

SUNDAY   DATE:

MEALS	READINGS	BEFORE	AFTER	NOTES
	BREAKFAST			
	LUNCH			
	DINNER			
	SNACKS			
	BEDTIME			

MONDAY   DATE:

MEALS	READINGS	BEFORE	AFTER	NOTES
	BREAKFAST			
	LUNCH			
	DINNER			
	SNACKS			
	BEDTIME			

TUESDAY   DATE:

MEALS	READINGS	BEFORE	AFTER	NOTES
	BREAKFAST			
	LUNCH			
	DINNER			
	SNACKS			
	BEDTIME			

WEDNESDAY   DATE:

MEALS	READINGS	BEFORE	AFTER	NOTES
	BREAKFAST			
	LUNCH			
	DINNER			
	SNACKS			
	BEDTIME			

THURSDAY   DATE:

MEALS	READINGS	BEFORE	AFTER	NOTES
	BREAKFAST			
	LUNCH			
	DINNER			
	SNACKS			
	BEDTIME			

FRIDAY   DATE:

MEALS	READINGS	BEFORE	AFTER	NOTES
	BREAKFAST			
	LUNCH			
	DINNER			
	SNACKS			
	BEDTIME			

SATURDAY   DATE:

MEALS	READINGS	BEFORE	AFTER	NOTES
	BREAKFAST			
	LUNCH			
	DINNER			
	SNACKS			
	BEDTIME			

NOTES

SUNDAY DATE:

MEALS	READINGS	BEFORE	AFTER	NOTES
	BREAKFAST			
	LUNCH			
	DINNER			
	SNACKS			
	BEDTIME			

MONDAY DATE:

MEALS	READINGS	BEFORE	AFTER	NOTES
	BREAKFAST			
	LUNCH			
	DINNER			
	SNACKS			
	BEDTIME			

TUESDAY DATE:

MEALS	READINGS	BEFORE	AFTER	NOTES
	BREAKFAST			
	LUNCH			
	DINNER			
	SNACKS			
	BEDTIME			

WEDNESDAY DATE:

MEALS	READINGS	BEFORE	AFTER	NOTES
	BREAKFAST			
	LUNCH			
	DINNER			
	SNACKS			
	BEDTIME			

THURSDAY   DATE:

MEALS	READINGS	BEFORE	AFTER	NOTES
	BREAKFAST			
	LUNCH			
	DINNER			
	SNACKS			
	BEDTIME			

FRIDAY   DATE:

MEALS	READINGS	BEFORE	AFTER	NOTES
	BREAKFAST			
	LUNCH			
	DINNER			
	SNACKS			
	BEDTIME			

SATURDAY   DATE:

MEALS	READINGS	BEFORE	AFTER	NOTES
	BREAKFAST			
	LUNCH			
	DINNER			
	SNACKS			
	BEDTIME			

NOTES

_____

_____

_____

_____

SUNDAY   DATE:

MEALS	READINGS	BEFORE	AFTER	NOTES
	BREAKFAST			
	LUNCH			
	DINNER			
	SNACKS			
	BEDTIME			

MONDAY   DATE:

MEALS	READINGS	BEFORE	AFTER	NOTES
	BREAKFAST			
	LUNCH			
	DINNER			
	SNACKS			
	BEDTIME			

TUESDAY   DATE:

MEALS	READINGS	BEFORE	AFTER	NOTES
	BREAKFAST			
	LUNCH			
	DINNER			
	SNACKS			
	BEDTIME			

WEDNESDAY   DATE:

MEALS	READINGS	BEFORE	AFTER	NOTES
	BREAKFAST			
	LUNCH			
	DINNER			
	SNACKS			
	BEDTIME			

THURSDAY   DATE:

MEALS	READINGS	BEFORE	AFTER	NOTES
	BREAKFAST			
	LUNCH			
	DINNER			
	SNACKS			
	BEDTIME			

FRIDAY   DATE:

MEALS	READINGS	BEFORE	AFTER	NOTES
	BREAKFAST			
	LUNCH			
	DINNER			
	SNACKS			
	BEDTIME			

SATURDAY   DATE:

MEALS	READINGS	BEFORE	AFTER	NOTES
	BREAKFAST			
	LUNCH			
	DINNER			
	SNACKS			
	BEDTIME			

NOTES

_____

_____

_____

_____

SUNDAY	DATE:			
MEALS	**READINGS**	**BEFORE**	**AFTER**	**NOTES**
	BREAKFAST			
	LUNCH			
	DINNER			
	SNACKS			
	BEDTIME			

MONDAY	DATE:			
MEALS	**READINGS**	**BEFORE**	**AFTER**	**NOTES**
	BREAKFAST			
	LUNCH			
	DINNER			
	SNACKS			
	BEDTIME			

TUESDAY	DATE:			
MEALS	**READINGS**	**BEFORE**	**AFTER**	**NOTES**
	BREAKFAST			
	LUNCH			
	DINNER			
	SNACKS			
	BEDTIME			

WEDNESDAY	DATE:			
MEALS	**READINGS**	**BEFORE**	**AFTER**	**NOTES**
	BREAKFAST			
	LUNCH			
	DINNER			
	SNACKS			
	BEDTIME			

THURSDAY		DATE:		
MEALS	**READINGS**	**BEFORE**	**AFTER**	**NOTES**
	BREAKFAST			
	LUNCH			
	DINNER			
	SNACKS			
	BEDTIME			

FRIDAY		DATE:		
MEALS	**READINGS**	**BEFORE**	**AFTER**	**NOTES**
	BREAKFAST			
	LUNCH			
	DINNER			
	SNACKS			
	BEDTIME			

SATURDAY		DATE:		
MEALS	**READINGS**	**BEFORE**	**AFTER**	**NOTES**
	BREAKFAST			
	LUNCH			
	DINNER			
	SNACKS			
	BEDTIME			

NOTES

_____

_____

_____

_____

SUNDAY   DATE:

MEALS	READINGS	BEFORE	AFTER	NOTES
	BREAKFAST			
	LUNCH			
	DINNER			
	SNACKS			
	BEDTIME			

MONDAY   DATE:

MEALS	READINGS	BEFORE	AFTER	NOTES
	BREAKFAST			
	LUNCH			
	DINNER			
	SNACKS			
	BEDTIME			

TUESDAY   DATE:

MEALS	READINGS	BEFORE	AFTER	NOTES
	BREAKFAST			
	LUNCH			
	DINNER			
	SNACKS			
	BEDTIME			

WEDNESDAY   DATE:

MEALS	READINGS	BEFORE	AFTER	NOTES
	BREAKFAST			
	LUNCH			
	DINNER			
	SNACKS			
	BEDTIME			

THURSDAY DATE:

MEALS	READINGS	BEFORE	AFTER	NOTES
	BREAKFAST			
	LUNCH			
	DINNER			
	SNACKS			
	BEDTIME			

FRIDAY DATE:

MEALS	READINGS	BEFORE	AFTER	NOTES
	BREAKFAST			
	LUNCH			
	DINNER			
	SNACKS			
	BEDTIME			

SATURDAY DATE:

MEALS	READINGS	BEFORE	AFTER	NOTES
	BREAKFAST			
	LUNCH			
	DINNER			
	SNACKS			
	BEDTIME			

NOTES

_____

_____

_____

_____

SUNDAY   DATE:

MEALS	READINGS	BEFORE	AFTER	NOTES
	BREAKFAST			
	LUNCH			
	DINNER			
	SNACKS			
	BEDTIME			

MONDAY   DATE:

MEALS	READINGS	BEFORE	AFTER	NOTES
	BREAKFAST			
	LUNCH			
	DINNER			
	SNACKS			
	BEDTIME			

TUESDAY   DATE:

MEALS	READINGS	BEFORE	AFTER	NOTES
	BREAKFAST			
	LUNCH			
	DINNER			
	SNACKS			
	BEDTIME			

WEDNESDAY   DATE:

MEALS	READINGS	BEFORE	AFTER	NOTES
	BREAKFAST			
	LUNCH			
	DINNER			
	SNACKS			
	BEDTIME			

THURSDAY		DATE:		
MEALS	**READINGS**	**BEFORE**	**AFTER**	**NOTES**
	BREAKFAST			
	LUNCH			
	DINNER			
	SNACKS			
	BEDTIME			

FRIDAY		DATE:		
MEALS	**READINGS**	**BEFORE**	**AFTER**	**NOTES**
	BREAKFAST			
	LUNCH			
	DINNER			
	SNACKS			
	BEDTIME			

SATURDAY		DATE:		
MEALS	**READINGS**	**BEFORE**	**AFTER**	**NOTES**
	BREAKFAST			
	LUNCH			
	DINNER			
	SNACKS			
	BEDTIME			

NOTES

_____

_____

_____

_____

SUNDAY DATE:

MEALS	READINGS	BEFORE	AFTER	NOTES
	BREAKFAST			
	LUNCH			
	DINNER			
	SNACKS			
	BEDTIME			

MONDAY DATE:

MEALS	READINGS	BEFORE	AFTER	NOTES
	BREAKFAST			
	LUNCH			
	DINNER			
	SNACKS			
	BEDTIME			

TUESDAY DATE:

MEALS	READINGS	BEFORE	AFTER	NOTES
	BREAKFAST			
	LUNCH			
	DINNER			
	SNACKS			
	BEDTIME			

WEDNESDAY DATE:

MEALS	READINGS	BEFORE	AFTER	NOTES
	BREAKFAST			
	LUNCH			
	DINNER			
	SNACKS			
	BEDTIME			

THURSDAY   DATE:

MEALS	READINGS	BEFORE	AFTER	NOTES
	BREAKFAST			
	LUNCH			
	DINNER			
	SNACKS			
	BEDTIME			

FRIDAY   DATE:

MEALS	READINGS	BEFORE	AFTER	NOTES
	BREAKFAST			
	LUNCH			
	DINNER			
	SNACKS			
	BEDTIME			

SATURDAY   DATE:

MEALS	READINGS	BEFORE	AFTER	NOTES
	BREAKFAST			
	LUNCH			
	DINNER			
	SNACKS			
	BEDTIME			

NOTES

_____

_____

_____

_____

SUNDAY   DATE:

MEALS	READINGS	BEFORE	AFTER	NOTES
	BREAKFAST			
	LUNCH			
	DINNER			
	SNACKS			
	BEDTIME			

MONDAY   DATE:

MEALS	READINGS	BEFORE	AFTER	NOTES
	BREAKFAST			
	LUNCH			
	DINNER			
	SNACKS			
	BEDTIME			

TUESDAY   DATE:

MEALS	READINGS	BEFORE	AFTER	NOTES
	BREAKFAST			
	LUNCH			
	DINNER			
	SNACKS			
	BEDTIME			

WEDNESDAY   DATE:

MEALS	READINGS	BEFORE	AFTER	NOTES
	BREAKFAST			
	LUNCH			
	DINNER			
	SNACKS			
	BEDTIME			

THURSDAY		DATE:		
MEALS	**READINGS**	**BEFORE**	**AFTER**	**NOTES**
	BREAKFAST			
	LUNCH			
	DINNER			
	SNACKS			
	BEDTIME			

FRIDAY		DATE:		
MEALS	**READINGS**	**BEFORE**	**AFTER**	**NOTES**
	BREAKFAST			
	LUNCH			
	DINNER			
	SNACKS			
	BEDTIME			

SATURDAY		DATE:		
MEALS	**READINGS**	**BEFORE**	**AFTER**	**NOTES**
	BREAKFAST			
	LUNCH			
	DINNER			
	SNACKS			
	BEDTIME			

NOTES

_____

_____

_____

_____

SUNDAY DATE:

MEALS	READINGS	BEFORE	AFTER	NOTES
	BREAKFAST			
	LUNCH			
	DINNER			
	SNACKS			
	BEDTIME			

MONDAY DATE:

MEALS	READINGS	BEFORE	AFTER	NOTES
	BREAKFAST			
	LUNCH			
	DINNER			
	SNACKS			
	BEDTIME			

TUESDAY DATE:

MEALS	READINGS	BEFORE	AFTER	NOTES
	BREAKFAST			
	LUNCH			
	DINNER			
	SNACKS			
	BEDTIME			

WEDNESDAY DATE:

MEALS	READINGS	BEFORE	AFTER	NOTES
	BREAKFAST			
	LUNCH			
	DINNER			
	SNACKS			
	BEDTIME			

THURSDAY DATE:

MEALS	READINGS	BEFORE	AFTER	NOTES
	BREAKFAST			
	LUNCH			
	DINNER			
	SNACKS			
	BEDTIME			

FRIDAY DATE:

MEALS	READINGS	BEFORE	AFTER	NOTES
	BREAKFAST			
	LUNCH			
	DINNER			
	SNACKS			
	BEDTIME			

SATURDAY DATE:

MEALS	READINGS	BEFORE	AFTER	NOTES
	BREAKFAST			
	LUNCH			
	DINNER			
	SNACKS			
	BEDTIME			

NOTES

_____

_____

_____

_____

SUNDAY   DATE:

MEALS	READINGS	BEFORE	AFTER	NOTES
	BREAKFAST			
	LUNCH			
	DINNER			
	SNACKS			
	BEDTIME			

MONDAY   DATE:

MEALS	READINGS	BEFORE	AFTER	NOTES
	BREAKFAST			
	LUNCH			
	DINNER			
	SNACKS			
	BEDTIME			

TUESDAY   DATE:

MEALS	READINGS	BEFORE	AFTER	NOTES
	BREAKFAST			
	LUNCH			
	DINNER			
	SNACKS			
	BEDTIME			

WEDNESDAY   DATE:

MEALS	READINGS	BEFORE	AFTER	NOTES
	BREAKFAST			
	LUNCH			
	DINNER			
	SNACKS			
	BEDTIME			

THURSDAY		DATE:		
MEALS	READINGS	BEFORE	AFTER	NOTES
	BREAKFAST			
	LUNCH			
	DINNER			
	SNACKS			
	BEDTIME			

FRIDAY		DATE:		
MEALS	READINGS	BEFORE	AFTER	NOTES
	BREAKFAST			
	LUNCH			
	DINNER			
	SNACKS			
	BEDTIME			

SATURDAY		DATE:		
MEALS	READINGS	BEFORE	AFTER	NOTES
	BREAKFAST			
	LUNCH			
	DINNER			
	SNACKS			
	BEDTIME			

NOTES

_____

_____

_____

_____

SUNDAY DATE:

MEALS	READINGS	BEFORE	AFTER	NOTES
	BREAKFAST			
	LUNCH			
	DINNER			
	SNACKS			
	BEDTIME			

MONDAY DATE:

MEALS	READINGS	BEFORE	AFTER	NOTES
	BREAKFAST			
	LUNCH			
	DINNER			
	SNACKS			
	BEDTIME			

TUESDAY DATE:

MEALS	READINGS	BEFORE	AFTER	NOTES
	BREAKFAST			
	LUNCH			
	DINNER			
	SNACKS			
	BEDTIME			

WEDNESDAY DATE:

MEALS	READINGS	BEFORE	AFTER	NOTES
	BREAKFAST			
	LUNCH			
	DINNER			
	SNACKS			
	BEDTIME			

THURSDAY   DATE:

MEALS	READINGS	BEFORE	AFTER	NOTES
	BREAKFAST			
	LUNCH			
	DINNER			
	SNACKS			
	BEDTIME			

FRIDAY   DATE:

MEALS	READINGS	BEFORE	AFTER	NOTES
	BREAKFAST			
	LUNCH			
	DINNER			
	SNACKS			
	BEDTIME			

SATURDAY   DATE:

MEALS	READINGS	BEFORE	AFTER	NOTES
	BREAKFAST			
	LUNCH			
	DINNER			
	SNACKS			
	BEDTIME			

NOTES

_____

_____

_____

_____

SUNDAY   DATE:

MEALS	READINGS	BEFORE	AFTER	NOTES
	BREAKFAST			
	LUNCH			
	DINNER			
	SNACKS			
	BEDTIME			

MONDAY   DATE:

MEALS	READINGS	BEFORE	AFTER	NOTES
	BREAKFAST			
	LUNCH			
	DINNER			
	SNACKS			
	BEDTIME			

TUESDAY   DATE:

MEALS	READINGS	BEFORE	AFTER	NOTES
	BREAKFAST			
	LUNCH			
	DINNER			
	SNACKS			
	BEDTIME			

WEDNESDAY   DATE:

MEALS	READINGS	BEFORE	AFTER	NOTES
	BREAKFAST			
	LUNCH			
	DINNER			
	SNACKS			
	BEDTIME			

THURSDAY DATE:

MEALS	READINGS	BEFORE	AFTER	NOTES
	BREAKFAST			
	LUNCH			
	DINNER			
	SNACKS			
	BEDTIME			

FRIDAY DATE:

MEALS	READINGS	BEFORE	AFTER	NOTES
	BREAKFAST			
	LUNCH			
	DINNER			
	SNACKS			
	BEDTIME			

SATURDAY DATE:

MEALS	READINGS	BEFORE	AFTER	NOTES
	BREAKFAST			
	LUNCH			
	DINNER			
	SNACKS			
	BEDTIME			

NOTES

_____

_____

_____

_____

SUNDAY		DATE:		
MEALS	**READINGS**	**BEFORE**	**AFTER**	**NOTES**
	BREAKFAST			
	LUNCH			
	DINNER			
	SNACKS			
	BEDTIME			

MONDAY		DATE:		
MEALS	**READINGS**	**BEFORE**	**AFTER**	**NOTES**
	BREAKFAST			
	LUNCH			
	DINNER			
	SNACKS			
	BEDTIME			

TUESDAY		DATE:		
MEALS	**READINGS**	**BEFORE**	**AFTER**	**NOTES**
	BREAKFAST			
	LUNCH			
	DINNER			
	SNACKS			
	BEDTIME			

WEDNESDAY		DATE:		
MEALS	**READINGS**	**BEFORE**	**AFTER**	**NOTES**
	BREAKFAST			
	LUNCH			
	DINNER			
	SNACKS			
	BEDTIME			

THURSDAY   DATE:

MEALS	READINGS	BEFORE	AFTER	NOTES
	BREAKFAST			
	LUNCH			
	DINNER			
	SNACKS			
	BEDTIME			

FRIDAY   DATE:

MEALS	READINGS	BEFORE	AFTER	NOTES
	BREAKFAST			
	LUNCH			
	DINNER			
	SNACKS			
	BEDTIME			

SATURDAY   DATE:

MEALS	READINGS	BEFORE	AFTER	NOTES
	BREAKFAST			
	LUNCH			
	DINNER			
	SNACKS			
	BEDTIME			

NOTES

_____

_____

_____

_____

SUNDAY   DATE:

MEALS	READINGS	BEFORE	AFTER	NOTES
	BREAKFAST			
	LUNCH			
	DINNER			
	SNACKS			
	BEDTIME			

MONDAY   DATE:

MEALS	READINGS	BEFORE	AFTER	NOTES
	BREAKFAST			
	LUNCH			
	DINNER			
	SNACKS			
	BEDTIME			

TUESDAY   DATE:

MEALS	READINGS	BEFORE	AFTER	NOTES
	BREAKFAST			
	LUNCH			
	DINNER			
	SNACKS			
	BEDTIME			

WEDNESDAY   DATE:

MEALS	READINGS	BEFORE	AFTER	NOTES
	BREAKFAST			
	LUNCH			
	DINNER			
	SNACKS			
	BEDTIME			

THURSDAY   DATE:

MEALS	READINGS	BEFORE	AFTER	NOTES
	BREAKFAST			
	LUNCH			
	DINNER			
	SNACKS			
	BEDTIME			

FRIDAY   DATE:

MEALS	READINGS	BEFORE	AFTER	NOTES
	BREAKFAST			
	LUNCH			
	DINNER			
	SNACKS			
	BEDTIME			

SATURDAY   DATE:

MEALS	READINGS	BEFORE	AFTER	NOTES
	BREAKFAST			
	LUNCH			
	DINNER			
	SNACKS			
	BEDTIME			

NOTES

_____

_____

_____

_____

SUNDAY		DATE:		
MEALS	**READINGS**	**BEFORE**	**AFTER**	**NOTES**
	BREAKFAST			
	LUNCH			
	DINNER			
	SNACKS			
	BEDTIME			

MONDAY		DATE:		
MEALS	**READINGS**	**BEFORE**	**AFTER**	**NOTES**
	BREAKFAST			
	LUNCH			
	DINNER			
	SNACKS			
	BEDTIME			

TUESDAY		DATE:		
MEALS	**READINGS**	**BEFORE**	**AFTER**	**NOTES**
	BREAKFAST			
	LUNCH			
	DINNER			
	SNACKS			
	BEDTIME			

WEDNESDAY		DATE:		
MEALS	**READINGS**	**BEFORE**	**AFTER**	**NOTES**
	BREAKFAST			
	LUNCH			
	DINNER			
	SNACKS			
	BEDTIME			

THURSDAY DATE:

MEALS	READINGS	BEFORE	AFTER	NOTES
	BREAKFAST			
	LUNCH			
	DINNER			
	SNACKS			
	BEDTIME			

FRIDAY DATE:

MEALS	READINGS	BEFORE	AFTER	NOTES
	BREAKFAST			
	LUNCH			
	DINNER			
	SNACKS			
	BEDTIME			

SATURDAY DATE:

MEALS	READINGS	BEFORE	AFTER	NOTES
	BREAKFAST			
	LUNCH			
	DINNER			
	SNACKS			
	BEDTIME			

NOTES

_____

_____

_____

_____

SUNDAY	DATE:			
MEALS	**READINGS**	**BEFORE**	**AFTER**	**NOTES**
	BREAKFAST			
	LUNCH			
	DINNER			
	SNACKS			
	BEDTIME			

MONDAY	DATE:			
MEALS	**READINGS**	**BEFORE**	**AFTER**	**NOTES**
	BREAKFAST			
	LUNCH			
	DINNER			
	SNACKS			
	BEDTIME			

TUESDAY	DATE:			
MEALS	**READINGS**	**BEFORE**	**AFTER**	**NOTES**
	BREAKFAST			
	LUNCH			
	DINNER			
	SNACKS			
	BEDTIME			

WEDNESDAY	DATE:			
MEALS	**READINGS**	**BEFORE**	**AFTER**	**NOTES**
	BREAKFAST			
	LUNCH			
	DINNER			
	SNACKS			
	BEDTIME			

THURSDAY   DATE:

MEALS	READINGS	BEFORE	AFTER	NOTES
	BREAKFAST			
	LUNCH			
	DINNER			
	SNACKS			
	BEDTIME			

FRIDAY   DATE:

MEALS	READINGS	BEFORE	AFTER	NOTES
	BREAKFAST			
	LUNCH			
	DINNER			
	SNACKS			
	BEDTIME			

SATURDAY   DATE:

MEALS	READINGS	BEFORE	AFTER	NOTES
	BREAKFAST			
	LUNCH			
	DINNER			
	SNACKS			
	BEDTIME			

NOTES

SUNDAY		DATE:		
MEALS	**READINGS**	**BEFORE**	**AFTER**	**NOTES**
	BREAKFAST			
	LUNCH			
	DINNER			
	SNACKS			
	BEDTIME			

MONDAY		DATE:		
MEALS	**READINGS**	**BEFORE**	**AFTER**	**NOTES**
	BREAKFAST			
	LUNCH			
	DINNER			
	SNACKS			
	BEDTIME			

TUESDAY		DATE:		
MEALS	**READINGS**	**BEFORE**	**AFTER**	**NOTES**
	BREAKFAST			
	LUNCH			
	DINNER			
	SNACKS			
	BEDTIME			

WEDNESDAY		DATE:		
MEALS	**READINGS**	**BEFORE**	**AFTER**	**NOTES**
	BREAKFAST			
	LUNCH			
	DINNER			
	SNACKS			
	BEDTIME			

THURSDAY		DATE:		

MEALS	READINGS	BEFORE	AFTER	NOTES
	BREAKFAST			
	LUNCH			
	DINNER			
	SNACKS			
	BEDTIME			

FRIDAY		DATE:		

MEALS	READINGS	BEFORE	AFTER	NOTES
	BREAKFAST			
	LUNCH			
	DINNER			
	SNACKS			
	BEDTIME			

SATURDAY		DATE:		

MEALS	READINGS	BEFORE	AFTER	NOTES
	BREAKFAST			
	LUNCH			
	DINNER			
	SNACKS			
	BEDTIME			

NOTES

_____

_____

_____

_____

SUNDAY DATE:

MEALS	READINGS	BEFORE	AFTER	NOTES
	BREAKFAST			
	LUNCH			
	DINNER			
	SNACKS			
	BEDTIME			

MONDAY DATE:

MEALS	READINGS	BEFORE	AFTER	NOTES
	BREAKFAST			
	LUNCH			
	DINNER			
	SNACKS			
	BEDTIME			

TUESDAY DATE:

MEALS	READINGS	BEFORE	AFTER	NOTES
	BREAKFAST			
	LUNCH			
	DINNER			
	SNACKS			
	BEDTIME			

WEDNESDAY DATE:

MEALS	READINGS	BEFORE	AFTER	NOTES
	BREAKFAST			
	LUNCH			
	DINNER			
	SNACKS			
	BEDTIME			

THURSDAY   DATE:

MEALS	READINGS	BEFORE	AFTER	NOTES
	BREAKFAST			
	LUNCH			
	DINNER			
	SNACKS			
	BEDTIME			

FRIDAY   DATE:

MEALS	READINGS	BEFORE	AFTER	NOTES
	BREAKFAST			
	LUNCH			
	DINNER			
	SNACKS			
	BEDTIME			

SATURDAY   DATE:

MEALS	READINGS	BEFORE	AFTER	NOTES
	BREAKFAST			
	LUNCH			
	DINNER			
	SNACKS			
	BEDTIME			

NOTES

_____

_____

_____

_____

SUNDAY   DATE:

MEALS	READINGS	BEFORE	AFTER	NOTES
	BREAKFAST			
	LUNCH			
	DINNER			
	SNACKS			
	BEDTIME			

MONDAY   DATE:

MEALS	READINGS	BEFORE	AFTER	NOTES
	BREAKFAST			
	LUNCH			
	DINNER			
	SNACKS			
	BEDTIME			

TUESDAY   DATE:

MEALS	READINGS	BEFORE	AFTER	NOTES
	BREAKFAST			
	LUNCH			
	DINNER			
	SNACKS			
	BEDTIME			

WEDNESDAY   DATE:

MEALS	READINGS	BEFORE	AFTER	NOTES
	BREAKFAST			
	LUNCH			
	DINNER			
	SNACKS			
	BEDTIME			

THURSDAY   DATE:

MEALS	READINGS	BEFORE	AFTER	NOTES
	BREAKFAST			
	LUNCH			
	DINNER			
	SNACKS			
	BEDTIME			

FRIDAY   DATE:

MEALS	READINGS	BEFORE	AFTER	NOTES
	BREAKFAST			
	LUNCH			
	DINNER			
	SNACKS			
	BEDTIME			

SATURDAY   DATE:

MEALS	READINGS	BEFORE	AFTER	NOTES
	BREAKFAST			
	LUNCH			
	DINNER			
	SNACKS			
	BEDTIME			

NOTES

_____

_____

_____

_____

SUNDAY DATE:

MEALS	READINGS	BEFORE	AFTER	NOTES
	BREAKFAST			
	LUNCH			
	DINNER			
	SNACKS			
	BEDTIME			

MONDAY DATE:

MEALS	READINGS	BEFORE	AFTER	NOTES
	BREAKFAST			
	LUNCH			
	DINNER			
	SNACKS			
	BEDTIME			

TUESDAY DATE:

MEALS	READINGS	BEFORE	AFTER	NOTES
	BREAKFAST			
	LUNCH			
	DINNER			
	SNACKS			
	BEDTIME			

WEDNESDAY DATE:

MEALS	READINGS	BEFORE	AFTER	NOTES
	BREAKFAST			
	LUNCH			
	DINNER			
	SNACKS			
	BEDTIME			

THURSDAY		DATE:		
MEALS	**READINGS**	**BEFORE**	**AFTER**	**NOTES**
	BREAKFAST			
	LUNCH			
	DINNER			
	SNACKS			
	BEDTIME			

FRIDAY		DATE:		
MEALS	**READINGS**	**BEFORE**	**AFTER**	**NOTES**
	BREAKFAST			
	LUNCH			
	DINNER			
	SNACKS			
	BEDTIME			

SATURDAY		DATE:		
MEALS	**READINGS**	**BEFORE**	**AFTER**	**NOTES**
	BREAKFAST			
	LUNCH			
	DINNER			
	SNACKS			
	BEDTIME			

NOTES

_____

_____

_____

_____

SUNDAY   DATE:

MEALS	READINGS	BEFORE	AFTER	NOTES
	BREAKFAST			
	LUNCH			
	DINNER			
	SNACKS			
	BEDTIME			

MONDAY   DATE:

MEALS	READINGS	BEFORE	AFTER	NOTES
	BREAKFAST			
	LUNCH			
	DINNER			
	SNACKS			
	BEDTIME			

TUESDAY   DATE:

MEALS	READINGS	BEFORE	AFTER	NOTES
	BREAKFAST			
	LUNCH			
	DINNER			
	SNACKS			
	BEDTIME			

WEDNESDAY   DATE:

MEALS	READINGS	BEFORE	AFTER	NOTES
	BREAKFAST			
	LUNCH			
	DINNER			
	SNACKS			
	BEDTIME			

THURSDAY   DATE:

MEALS	READINGS	BEFORE	AFTER	NOTES
	BREAKFAST			
	LUNCH			
	DINNER			
	SNACKS			
	BEDTIME			

FRIDAY   DATE:

MEALS	READINGS	BEFORE	AFTER	NOTES
	BREAKFAST			
	LUNCH			
	DINNER			
	SNACKS			
	BEDTIME			

SATURDAY   DATE:

MEALS	READINGS	BEFORE	AFTER	NOTES
	BREAKFAST			
	LUNCH			
	DINNER			
	SNACKS			
	BEDTIME			

NOTES

_____

_____

_____

_____

SUNDAY		DATE:		
MEALS	**READINGS**	**BEFORE**	**AFTER**	**NOTES**
	BREAKFAST			
	LUNCH			
	DINNER			
	SNACKS			
	BEDTIME			

MONDAY		DATE:		
MEALS	**READINGS**	**BEFORE**	**AFTER**	**NOTES**
	BREAKFAST			
	LUNCH			
	DINNER			
	SNACKS			
	BEDTIME			

TUESDAY		DATE:		
MEALS	**READINGS**	**BEFORE**	**AFTER**	**NOTES**
	BREAKFAST			
	LUNCH			
	DINNER			
	SNACKS			
	BEDTIME			

WEDNESDAY		DATE:		
MEALS	**READINGS**	**BEFORE**	**AFTER**	**NOTES**
	BREAKFAST			
	LUNCH			
	DINNER			
	SNACKS			
	BEDTIME			

THURSDAY   DATE:

MEALS	READINGS	BEFORE	AFTER	NOTES
	BREAKFAST			
	LUNCH			
	DINNER			
	SNACKS			
	BEDTIME			

FRIDAY   DATE:

MEALS	READINGS	BEFORE	AFTER	NOTES
	BREAKFAST			
	LUNCH			
	DINNER			
	SNACKS			
	BEDTIME			

SATURDAY   DATE:

MEALS	READINGS	BEFORE	AFTER	NOTES
	BREAKFAST			
	LUNCH			
	DINNER			
	SNACKS			
	BEDTIME			

NOTES

_____

_____

_____

_____

SUNDAY		DATE:		
MEALS	**READINGS**	**BEFORE**	**AFTER**	**NOTES**
	BREAKFAST			
	LUNCH			
	DINNER			
	SNACKS			
	BEDTIME			

MONDAY		DATE:		
MEALS	**READINGS**	**BEFORE**	**AFTER**	**NOTES**
	BREAKFAST			
	LUNCH			
	DINNER			
	SNACKS			
	BEDTIME			

TUESDAY		DATE:		
MEALS	**READINGS**	**BEFORE**	**AFTER**	**NOTES**
	BREAKFAST			
	LUNCH			
	DINNER			
	SNACKS			
	BEDTIME			

WEDNESDAY		DATE:		
MEALS	**READINGS**	**BEFORE**	**AFTER**	**NOTES**
	BREAKFAST			
	LUNCH			
	DINNER			
	SNACKS			
	BEDTIME			

THURSDAY — DATE:

MEALS	READINGS	BEFORE	AFTER	NOTES
	BREAKFAST			
	LUNCH			
	DINNER			
	SNACKS			
	BEDTIME			

FRIDAY — DATE:

MEALS	READINGS	BEFORE	AFTER	NOTES
	BREAKFAST			
	LUNCH			
	DINNER			
	SNACKS			
	BEDTIME			

SATURDAY — DATE:

MEALS	READINGS	BEFORE	AFTER	NOTES
	BREAKFAST			
	LUNCH			
	DINNER			
	SNACKS			
	BEDTIME			

NOTES

_____

_____

_____

_____

SUNDAY		DATE:		
MEALS	**READINGS**	**BEFORE**	**AFTER**	**NOTES**
	BREAKFAST			
	LUNCH			
	DINNER			
	SNACKS			
	BEDTIME			

MONDAY		DATE:		
MEALS	**READINGS**	**BEFORE**	**AFTER**	**NOTES**
	BREAKFAST			
	LUNCH			
	DINNER			
	SNACKS			
	BEDTIME			

TUESDAY		DATE:		
MEALS	**READINGS**	**BEFORE**	**AFTER**	**NOTES**
	BREAKFAST			
	LUNCH			
	DINNER			
	SNACKS			
	BEDTIME			

WEDNESDAY		DATE:		
MEALS	**READINGS**	**BEFORE**	**AFTER**	**NOTES**
	BREAKFAST			
	LUNCH			
	DINNER			
	SNACKS			
	BEDTIME			

THURSDAY		DATE:		
MEALS	READINGS	BEFORE	AFTER	NOTES
	BREAKFAST			
	LUNCH			
	DINNER			
	SNACKS			
	BEDTIME			

FRIDAY		DATE:		
MEALS	READINGS	BEFORE	AFTER	NOTES
	BREAKFAST			
	LUNCH			
	DINNER			
	SNACKS			
	BEDTIME			

SATURDAY		DATE:		
MEALS	READINGS	BEFORE	AFTER	NOTES
	BREAKFAST			
	LUNCH			
	DINNER			
	SNACKS			
	BEDTIME			

NOTES

_____

_____

_____

_____

SUNDAY DATE:

MEALS	READINGS	BEFORE	AFTER	NOTES
	BREAKFAST			
	LUNCH			
	DINNER			
	SNACKS			
	BEDTIME			

MONDAY DATE:

MEALS	READINGS	BEFORE	AFTER	NOTES
	BREAKFAST			
	LUNCH			
	DINNER			
	SNACKS			
	BEDTIME			

TUESDAY DATE:

MEALS	READINGS	BEFORE	AFTER	NOTES
	BREAKFAST			
	LUNCH			
	DINNER			
	SNACKS			
	BEDTIME			

WEDNESDAY DATE:

MEALS	READINGS	BEFORE	AFTER	NOTES
	BREAKFAST			
	LUNCH			
	DINNER			
	SNACKS			
	BEDTIME			

THURSDAY DATE:

MEALS	READINGS	BEFORE	AFTER	NOTES
	BREAKFAST			
	LUNCH			
	DINNER			
	SNACKS			
	BEDTIME			

FRIDAY DATE:

MEALS	READINGS	BEFORE	AFTER	NOTES
	BREAKFAST			
	LUNCH			
	DINNER			
	SNACKS			
	BEDTIME			

SATURDAY DATE:

MEALS	READINGS	BEFORE	AFTER	NOTES
	BREAKFAST			
	LUNCH			
	DINNER			
	SNACKS			
	BEDTIME			

NOTES

_____

_____

_____

_____

SUNDAY   DATE:

MEALS	READINGS	BEFORE	AFTER	NOTES
	BREAKFAST			
	LUNCH			
	DINNER			
	SNACKS			
	BEDTIME			

MONDAY   DATE:

MEALS	READINGS	BEFORE	AFTER	NOTES
	BREAKFAST			
	LUNCH			
	DINNER			
	SNACKS			
	BEDTIME			

TUESDAY   DATE:

MEALS	READINGS	BEFORE	AFTER	NOTES
	BREAKFAST			
	LUNCH			
	DINNER			
	SNACKS			
	BEDTIME			

WEDNESDAY   DATE:

MEALS	READINGS	BEFORE	AFTER	NOTES
	BREAKFAST			
	LUNCH			
	DINNER			
	SNACKS			
	BEDTIME			

THURSDAY   DATE:

MEALS	READINGS	BEFORE	AFTER	NOTES
	BREAKFAST			
	LUNCH			
	DINNER			
	SNACKS			
	BEDTIME			

FRIDAY   DATE:

MEALS	READINGS	BEFORE	AFTER	NOTES
	BREAKFAST			
	LUNCH			
	DINNER			
	SNACKS			
	BEDTIME			

SATURDAY   DATE:

MEALS	READINGS	BEFORE	AFTER	NOTES
	BREAKFAST			
	LUNCH			
	DINNER			
	SNACKS			
	BEDTIME			

NOTES

_____

_____

_____

_____

SUNDAY   DATE:

MEALS	READINGS	BEFORE	AFTER	NOTES
	BREAKFAST			
	LUNCH			
	DINNER			
	SNACKS			
	BEDTIME			

MONDAY   DATE:

MEALS	READINGS	BEFORE	AFTER	NOTES
	BREAKFAST			
	LUNCH			
	DINNER			
	SNACKS			
	BEDTIME			

TUESDAY   DATE:

MEALS	READINGS	BEFORE	AFTER	NOTES
	BREAKFAST			
	LUNCH			
	DINNER			
	SNACKS			
	BEDTIME			

WEDNESDAY   DATE:

MEALS	READINGS	BEFORE	AFTER	NOTES
	BREAKFAST			
	LUNCH			
	DINNER			
	SNACKS			
	BEDTIME			

THURSDAY   DATE:

MEALS	READINGS	BEFORE	AFTER	NOTES
	BREAKFAST			
	LUNCH			
	DINNER			
	SNACKS			
	BEDTIME			

FRIDAY   DATE:

MEALS	READINGS	BEFORE	AFTER	NOTES
	BREAKFAST			
	LUNCH			
	DINNER			
	SNACKS			
	BEDTIME			

SATURDAY   DATE:

MEALS	READINGS	BEFORE	AFTER	NOTES
	BREAKFAST			
	LUNCH			
	DINNER			
	SNACKS			
	BEDTIME			

NOTES

_____

_____

_____

_____

SUNDAY DATE:

MEALS	READINGS	BEFORE	AFTER	NOTES
	BREAKFAST			
	LUNCH			
	DINNER			
	SNACKS			
	BEDTIME			

MONDAY DATE:

MEALS	READINGS	BEFORE	AFTER	NOTES
	BREAKFAST			
	LUNCH			
	DINNER			
	SNACKS			
	BEDTIME			

TUESDAY DATE:

MEALS	READINGS	BEFORE	AFTER	NOTES
	BREAKFAST			
	LUNCH			
	DINNER			
	SNACKS			
	BEDTIME			

WEDNESDAY DATE:

MEALS	READINGS	BEFORE	AFTER	NOTES
	BREAKFAST			
	LUNCH			
	DINNER			
	SNACKS			
	BEDTIME			

THURSDAY		DATE:		
MEALS	**READINGS**	**BEFORE**	**AFTER**	**NOTES**
	BREAKFAST			
	LUNCH			
	DINNER			
	SNACKS			
	BEDTIME			

FRIDAY		DATE:		
MEALS	**READINGS**	**BEFORE**	**AFTER**	**NOTES**
	BREAKFAST			
	LUNCH			
	DINNER			
	SNACKS			
	BEDTIME			

SATURDAY		DATE:		
MEALS	**READINGS**	**BEFORE**	**AFTER**	**NOTES**
	BREAKFAST			
	LUNCH			
	DINNER			
	SNACKS			
	BEDTIME			

NOTES

_____

_____

_____

_____

SUNDAY		DATE:		
MEALS	**READINGS**	**BEFORE**	**AFTER**	**NOTES**
	BREAKFAST			
	LUNCH			
	DINNER			
	SNACKS			
	BEDTIME			

MONDAY		DATE:		
MEALS	**READINGS**	**BEFORE**	**AFTER**	**NOTES**
	BREAKFAST			
	LUNCH			
	DINNER			
	SNACKS			
	BEDTIME			

TUESDAY		DATE:		
MEALS	**READINGS**	**BEFORE**	**AFTER**	**NOTES**
	BREAKFAST			
	LUNCH			
	DINNER			
	SNACKS			
	BEDTIME			

WEDNESDAY		DATE:		
MEALS	**READINGS**	**BEFORE**	**AFTER**	**NOTES**
	BREAKFAST			
	LUNCH			
	DINNER			
	SNACKS			
	BEDTIME			

THURSDAY		DATE:		
MEALS	**READINGS**	**BEFORE**	**AFTER**	**NOTES**
	BREAKFAST			
	LUNCH			
	DINNER			
	SNACKS			
	BEDTIME			

FRIDAY		DATE:		
MEALS	**READINGS**	**BEFORE**	**AFTER**	**NOTES**
	BREAKFAST			
	LUNCH			
	DINNER			
	SNACKS			
	BEDTIME			

SATURDAY		DATE:		
MEALS	**READINGS**	**BEFORE**	**AFTER**	**NOTES**
	BREAKFAST			
	LUNCH			
	DINNER			
	SNACKS			
	BEDTIME			

NOTES

_____

_____

_____

_____

SUNDAY		DATE:		
MEALS	**READINGS**	**BEFORE**	**AFTER**	**NOTES**
	BREAKFAST			
	LUNCH			
	DINNER			
	SNACKS			
	BEDTIME			

MONDAY		DATE:		
MEALS	**READINGS**	**BEFORE**	**AFTER**	**NOTES**
	BREAKFAST			
	LUNCH			
	DINNER			
	SNACKS			
	BEDTIME			

TUESDAY		DATE:		
MEALS	**READINGS**	**BEFORE**	**AFTER**	**NOTES**
	BREAKFAST			
	LUNCH			
	DINNER			
	SNACKS			
	BEDTIME			

WEDNESDAY		DATE:		
MEALS	**READINGS**	**BEFORE**	**AFTER**	**NOTES**
	BREAKFAST			
	LUNCH			
	DINNER			
	SNACKS			
	BEDTIME			

THURSDAY — DATE:

MEALS	READINGS	BEFORE	AFTER	NOTES
	BREAKFAST			
	LUNCH			
	DINNER			
	SNACKS			
	BEDTIME			

FRIDAY — DATE:

MEALS	READINGS	BEFORE	AFTER	NOTES
	BREAKFAST			
	LUNCH			
	DINNER			
	SNACKS			
	BEDTIME			

SATURDAY — DATE:

MEALS	READINGS	BEFORE	AFTER	NOTES
	BREAKFAST			
	LUNCH			
	DINNER			
	SNACKS			
	BEDTIME			

NOTES

SUNDAY   DATE:

MEALS	READINGS	BEFORE	AFTER	NOTES
	BREAKFAST			
	LUNCH			
	DINNER			
	SNACKS			
	BEDTIME			

MONDAY   DATE:

MEALS	READINGS	BEFORE	AFTER	NOTES
	BREAKFAST			
	LUNCH			
	DINNER			
	SNACKS			
	BEDTIME			

TUESDAY   DATE:

MEALS	READINGS	BEFORE	AFTER	NOTES
	BREAKFAST			
	LUNCH			
	DINNER			
	SNACKS			
	BEDTIME			

WEDNESDAY   DATE:

MEALS	READINGS	BEFORE	AFTER	NOTES
	BREAKFAST			
	LUNCH			
	DINNER			
	SNACKS			
	BEDTIME			

THURSDAY		DATE:		
MEALS	READINGS	BEFORE	AFTER	NOTES
	BREAKFAST			
	LUNCH			
	DINNER			
	SNACKS			
	BEDTIME			

FRIDAY		DATE:		
MEALS	READINGS	BEFORE	AFTER	NOTES
	BREAKFAST			
	LUNCH			
	DINNER			
	SNACKS			
	BEDTIME			

SATURDAY		DATE:		
MEALS	READINGS	BEFORE	AFTER	NOTES
	BREAKFAST			
	LUNCH			
	DINNER			
	SNACKS			
	BEDTIME			

NOTES

_____

_____

_____

_____

SUNDAY		DATE:		
MEALS	**READINGS**	**BEFORE**	**AFTER**	**NOTES**
	BREAKFAST			
	LUNCH			
	DINNER			
	SNACKS			
	BEDTIME			

MONDAY		DATE:		
MEALS	**READINGS**	**BEFORE**	**AFTER**	**NOTES**
	BREAKFAST			
	LUNCH			
	DINNER			
	SNACKS			
	BEDTIME			

TUESDAY		DATE:		
MEALS	**READINGS**	**BEFORE**	**AFTER**	**NOTES**
	BREAKFAST			
	LUNCH			
	DINNER			
	SNACKS			
	BEDTIME			

WEDNESDAY		DATE:		
MEALS	**READINGS**	**BEFORE**	**AFTER**	**NOTES**
	BREAKFAST			
	LUNCH			
	DINNER			
	SNACKS			
	BEDTIME			

THURSDAY   DATE:

MEALS	READINGS	BEFORE	AFTER	NOTES
	BREAKFAST			
	LUNCH			
	DINNER			
	SNACKS			
	BEDTIME			

FRIDAY   DATE:

MEALS	READINGS	BEFORE	AFTER	NOTES
	BREAKFAST			
	LUNCH			
	DINNER			
	SNACKS			
	BEDTIME			

SATURDAY   DATE:

MEALS	READINGS	BEFORE	AFTER	NOTES
	BREAKFAST			
	LUNCH			
	DINNER			
	SNACKS			
	BEDTIME			

NOTES

_____

_____

_____

_____

SUNDAY   DATE:

MEALS	READINGS	BEFORE	AFTER	NOTES
	BREAKFAST			
	LUNCH			
	DINNER			
	SNACKS			
	BEDTIME			

MONDAY   DATE:

MEALS	READINGS	BEFORE	AFTER	NOTES
	BREAKFAST			
	LUNCH			
	DINNER			
	SNACKS			
	BEDTIME			

TUESDAY   DATE:

MEALS	READINGS	BEFORE	AFTER	NOTES
	BREAKFAST			
	LUNCH			
	DINNER			
	SNACKS			
	BEDTIME			

WEDNESDAY   DATE:

MEALS	READINGS	BEFORE	AFTER	NOTES
	BREAKFAST			
	LUNCH			
	DINNER			
	SNACKS			
	BEDTIME			

THURSDAY		DATE:		
MEALS	**READINGS**	**BEFORE**	**AFTER**	**NOTES**
	BREAKFAST			
	LUNCH			
	DINNER			
	SNACKS			
	BEDTIME			

FRIDAY		DATE:		
MEALS	**READINGS**	**BEFORE**	**AFTER**	**NOTES**
	BREAKFAST			
	LUNCH			
	DINNER			
	SNACKS			
	BEDTIME			

SATURDAY		DATE:		
MEALS	**READINGS**	**BEFORE**	**AFTER**	**NOTES**
	BREAKFAST			
	LUNCH			
	DINNER			
	SNACKS			
	BEDTIME			

NOTES

_____

_____

_____

_____

SUNDAY   DATE:

MEALS	READINGS	BEFORE	AFTER	NOTES
	BREAKFAST			
	LUNCH			
	DINNER			
	SNACKS			
	BEDTIME			

MONDAY   DATE:

MEALS	READINGS	BEFORE	AFTER	NOTES
	BREAKFAST			
	LUNCH			
	DINNER			
	SNACKS			
	BEDTIME			

TUESDAY   DATE:

MEALS	READINGS	BEFORE	AFTER	NOTES
	BREAKFAST			
	LUNCH			
	DINNER			
	SNACKS			
	BEDTIME			

WEDNESDAY   DATE:

MEALS	READINGS	BEFORE	AFTER	NOTES
	BREAKFAST			
	LUNCH			
	DINNER			
	SNACKS			
	BEDTIME			

THURSDAY		DATE:		
MEALS	**READINGS**	**BEFORE**	**AFTER**	**NOTES**
	BREAKFAST			
	LUNCH			
	DINNER			
	SNACKS			
	BEDTIME			

FRIDAY		DATE:		
MEALS	**READINGS**	**BEFORE**	**AFTER**	**NOTES**
	BREAKFAST			
	LUNCH			
	DINNER			
	SNACKS			
	BEDTIME			

SATURDAY		DATE:		
MEALS	**READINGS**	**BEFORE**	**AFTER**	**NOTES**
	BREAKFAST			
	LUNCH			
	DINNER			
	SNACKS			
	BEDTIME			

NOTES

_____

_____

_____

_____

SUNDAY   DATE:

MEALS	READINGS	BEFORE	AFTER	NOTES
	BREAKFAST			
	LUNCH			
	DINNER			
	SNACKS			
	BEDTIME			

MONDAY   DATE:

MEALS	READINGS	BEFORE	AFTER	NOTES
	BREAKFAST			
	LUNCH			
	DINNER			
	SNACKS			
	BEDTIME			

TUESDAY   DATE:

MEALS	READINGS	BEFORE	AFTER	NOTES
	BREAKFAST			
	LUNCH			
	DINNER			
	SNACKS			
	BEDTIME			

WEDNESDAY   DATE:

MEALS	READINGS	BEFORE	AFTER	NOTES
	BREAKFAST			
	LUNCH			
	DINNER			
	SNACKS			
	BEDTIME			

THURSDAY		DATE:		
MEALS	**READINGS**	**BEFORE**	**AFTER**	**NOTES**
	BREAKFAST			
	LUNCH			
	DINNER			
	SNACKS			
	BEDTIME			

FRIDAY		DATE:		
MEALS	**READINGS**	**BEFORE**	**AFTER**	**NOTES**
	BREAKFAST			
	LUNCH			
	DINNER			
	SNACKS			
	BEDTIME			

SATURDAY		DATE:		
MEALS	**READINGS**	**BEFORE**	**AFTER**	**NOTES**
	BREAKFAST			
	LUNCH			
	DINNER			
	SNACKS			
	BEDTIME			

NOTES

_____

_____

_____

_____

SUNDAY DATE:

MEALS	READINGS	BEFORE	AFTER	NOTES
	BREAKFAST			
	LUNCH			
	DINNER			
	SNACKS			
	BEDTIME			

MONDAY DATE:

MEALS	READINGS	BEFORE	AFTER	NOTES
	BREAKFAST			
	LUNCH			
	DINNER			
	SNACKS			
	BEDTIME			

TUESDAY DATE:

MEALS	READINGS	BEFORE	AFTER	NOTES
	BREAKFAST			
	LUNCH			
	DINNER			
	SNACKS			
	BEDTIME			

WEDNESDAY DATE:

MEALS	READINGS	BEFORE	AFTER	NOTES
	BREAKFAST			
	LUNCH			
	DINNER			
	SNACKS			
	BEDTIME			

THURSDAY   DATE:

MEALS	READINGS	BEFORE	AFTER	NOTES
	BREAKFAST			
	LUNCH			
	DINNER			
	SNACKS			
	BEDTIME			

FRIDAY   DATE:

MEALS	READINGS	BEFORE	AFTER	NOTES
	BREAKFAST			
	LUNCH			
	DINNER			
	SNACKS			
	BEDTIME			

SATURDAY   DATE:

MEALS	READINGS	BEFORE	AFTER	NOTES
	BREAKFAST			
	LUNCH			
	DINNER			
	SNACKS			
	BEDTIME			

NOTES

_____

_____

_____

_____

SUNDAY   DATE:

MEALS	READINGS	BEFORE	AFTER	NOTES
	BREAKFAST			
	LUNCH			
	DINNER			
	SNACKS			
	BEDTIME			

MONDAY   DATE:

MEALS	READINGS	BEFORE	AFTER	NOTES
	BREAKFAST			
	LUNCH			
	DINNER			
	SNACKS			
	BEDTIME			

TUESDAY   DATE:

MEALS	READINGS	BEFORE	AFTER	NOTES
	BREAKFAST			
	LUNCH			
	DINNER			
	SNACKS			
	BEDTIME			

WEDNESDAY   DATE:

MEALS	READINGS	BEFORE	AFTER	NOTES
	BREAKFAST			
	LUNCH			
	DINNER			
	SNACKS			
	BEDTIME			

THURSDAY	DATE:			
MEALS	**READINGS**	**BEFORE**	**AFTER**	**NOTES**
	BREAKFAST			
	LUNCH			
	DINNER			
	SNACKS			
	BEDTIME			

FRIDAY	DATE:			
MEALS	**READINGS**	**BEFORE**	**AFTER**	**NOTES**
	BREAKFAST			
	LUNCH			
	DINNER			
	SNACKS			
	BEDTIME			

SATURDAY	DATE:			
MEALS	**READINGS**	**BEFORE**	**AFTER**	**NOTES**
	BREAKFAST			
	LUNCH			
	DINNER			
	SNACKS			
	BEDTIME			

NOTES

_____

_____

_____

_____

SUNDAY DATE:

MEALS	READINGS	BEFORE	AFTER	NOTES
	BREAKFAST			
	LUNCH			
	DINNER			
	SNACKS			
	BEDTIME			

MONDAY DATE:

MEALS	READINGS	BEFORE	AFTER	NOTES
	BREAKFAST			
	LUNCH			
	DINNER			
	SNACKS			
	BEDTIME			

TUESDAY DATE:

MEALS	READINGS	BEFORE	AFTER	NOTES
	BREAKFAST			
	LUNCH			
	DINNER			
	SNACKS			
	BEDTIME			

WEDNESDAY DATE:

MEALS	READINGS	BEFORE	AFTER	NOTES
	BREAKFAST			
	LUNCH			
	DINNER			
	SNACKS			
	BEDTIME			

THURSDAY	DATE:			
MEALS	**READINGS**	**BEFORE**	**AFTER**	**NOTES**
	BREAKFAST			
	LUNCH			
	DINNER			
	SNACKS			
	BEDTIME			

FRIDAY	DATE:			
MEALS	**READINGS**	**BEFORE**	**AFTER**	**NOTES**
	BREAKFAST			
	LUNCH			
	DINNER			
	SNACKS			
	BEDTIME			

SATURDAY	DATE:			
MEALS	**READINGS**	**BEFORE**	**AFTER**	**NOTES**
	BREAKFAST			
	LUNCH			
	DINNER			
	SNACKS			
	BEDTIME			

NOTES

_____

_____

_____

_____

SUNDAY   DATE:

MEALS	READINGS	BEFORE	AFTER	NOTES
	BREAKFAST			
	LUNCH			
	DINNER			
	SNACKS			
	BEDTIME			

MONDAY   DATE:

MEALS	READINGS	BEFORE	AFTER	NOTES
	BREAKFAST			
	LUNCH			
	DINNER			
	SNACKS			
	BEDTIME			

TUESDAY   DATE:

MEALS	READINGS	BEFORE	AFTER	NOTES
	BREAKFAST			
	LUNCH			
	DINNER			
	SNACKS			
	BEDTIME			

WEDNESDAY   DATE:

MEALS	READINGS	BEFORE	AFTER	NOTES
	BREAKFAST			
	LUNCH			
	DINNER			
	SNACKS			
	BEDTIME			

THURSDAY		DATE:		
MEALS	READINGS	BEFORE	AFTER	NOTES
	BREAKFAST			
	LUNCH			
	DINNER			
	SNACKS			
	BEDTIME			

FRIDAY		DATE:		
MEALS	READINGS	BEFORE	AFTER	NOTES
	BREAKFAST			
	LUNCH			
	DINNER			
	SNACKS			
	BEDTIME			

SATURDAY		DATE:		
MEALS	READINGS	BEFORE	AFTER	NOTES
	BREAKFAST			
	LUNCH			
	DINNER			
	SNACKS			
	BEDTIME			

NOTES

_____

_____

_____

_____

SUNDAY   DATE:

MEALS	READINGS	BEFORE	AFTER	NOTES
	BREAKFAST			
	LUNCH			
	DINNER			
	SNACKS			
	BEDTIME			

MONDAY   DATE:

MEALS	READINGS	BEFORE	AFTER	NOTES
	BREAKFAST			
	LUNCH			
	DINNER			
	SNACKS			
	BEDTIME			

TUESDAY   DATE:

MEALS	READINGS	BEFORE	AFTER	NOTES
	BREAKFAST			
	LUNCH			
	DINNER			
	SNACKS			
	BEDTIME			

WEDNESDAY   DATE:

MEALS	READINGS	BEFORE	AFTER	NOTES
	BREAKFAST			
	LUNCH			
	DINNER			
	SNACKS			
	BEDTIME			

THURSDAY		DATE:		
MEALS	**READINGS**	**BEFORE**	**AFTER**	**NOTES**
	BREAKFAST			
	LUNCH			
	DINNER			
	SNACKS			
	BEDTIME			

FRIDAY		DATE:		
MEALS	**READINGS**	**BEFORE**	**AFTER**	**NOTES**
	BREAKFAST			
	LUNCH			
	DINNER			
	SNACKS			
	BEDTIME			

SATURDAY		DATE:		
MEALS	**READINGS**	**BEFORE**	**AFTER**	**NOTES**
	BREAKFAST			
	LUNCH			
	DINNER			
	SNACKS			
	BEDTIME			

NOTES

_____

_____

_____

_____

SUNDAY — DATE:

MEALS	READINGS	BEFORE	AFTER	NOTES
	BREAKFAST			
	LUNCH			
	DINNER			
	SNACKS			
	BEDTIME			

MONDAY — DATE:

MEALS	READINGS	BEFORE	AFTER	NOTES
	BREAKFAST			
	LUNCH			
	DINNER			
	SNACKS			
	BEDTIME			

TUESDAY — DATE:

MEALS	READINGS	BEFORE	AFTER	NOTES
	BREAKFAST			
	LUNCH			
	DINNER			
	SNACKS			
	BEDTIME			

WEDNESDAY — DATE:

MEALS	READINGS	BEFORE	AFTER	NOTES
	BREAKFAST			
	LUNCH			
	DINNER			
	SNACKS			
	BEDTIME			

THURSDAY		DATE:		
MEALS	**READINGS**	**BEFORE**	**AFTER**	**NOTES**
	BREAKFAST			
	LUNCH			
	DINNER			
	SNACKS			
	BEDTIME			

FRIDAY		DATE:		
MEALS	**READINGS**	**BEFORE**	**AFTER**	**NOTES**
	BREAKFAST			
	LUNCH			
	DINNER			
	SNACKS			
	BEDTIME			

SATURDAY		DATE:		
MEALS	**READINGS**	**BEFORE**	**AFTER**	**NOTES**
	BREAKFAST			
	LUNCH			
	DINNER			
	SNACKS			
	BEDTIME			

NOTES

_____

_____

_____

_____

SUNDAY — DATE:

MEALS	READINGS	BEFORE	AFTER	NOTES
	BREAKFAST			
	LUNCH			
	DINNER			
	SNACKS			
	BEDTIME			

MONDAY — DATE:

MEALS	READINGS	BEFORE	AFTER	NOTES
	BREAKFAST			
	LUNCH			
	DINNER			
	SNACKS			
	BEDTIME			

TUESDAY — DATE:

MEALS	READINGS	BEFORE	AFTER	NOTES
	BREAKFAST			
	LUNCH			
	DINNER			
	SNACKS			
	BEDTIME			

WEDNESDAY — DATE:

MEALS	READINGS	BEFORE	AFTER	NOTES
	BREAKFAST			
	LUNCH			
	DINNER			
	SNACKS			
	BEDTIME			

THURSDAY   DATE:

MEALS	READINGS	BEFORE	AFTER	NOTES
	BREAKFAST			
	LUNCH			
	DINNER			
	SNACKS			
	BEDTIME			

FRIDAY   DATE:

MEALS	READINGS	BEFORE	AFTER	NOTES
	BREAKFAST			
	LUNCH			
	DINNER			
	SNACKS			
	BEDTIME			

SATURDAY   DATE:

MEALS	READINGS	BEFORE	AFTER	NOTES
	BREAKFAST			
	LUNCH			
	DINNER			
	SNACKS			
	BEDTIME			

NOTES

_____

_____

_____

_____

SUNDAY DATE:

MEALS	READINGS	BEFORE	AFTER	NOTES
	BREAKFAST			
	LUNCH			
	DINNER			
	SNACKS			
	BEDTIME			

MONDAY DATE:

MEALS	READINGS	BEFORE	AFTER	NOTES
	BREAKFAST			
	LUNCH			
	DINNER			
	SNACKS			
	BEDTIME			

TUESDAY DATE:

MEALS	READINGS	BEFORE	AFTER	NOTES
	BREAKFAST			
	LUNCH			
	DINNER			
	SNACKS			
	BEDTIME			

WEDNESDAY DATE:

MEALS	READINGS	BEFORE	AFTER	NOTES
	BREAKFAST			
	LUNCH			
	DINNER			
	SNACKS			
	BEDTIME			

THURSDAY		DATE:		
MEALS	READINGS	BEFORE	AFTER	NOTES
	BREAKFAST			
	LUNCH			
	DINNER			
	SNACKS			
	BEDTIME			

FRIDAY		DATE:		
MEALS	READINGS	BEFORE	AFTER	NOTES
	BREAKFAST			
	LUNCH			
	DINNER			
	SNACKS			
	BEDTIME			

SATURDAY		DATE:		
MEALS	READINGS	BEFORE	AFTER	NOTES
	BREAKFAST			
	LUNCH			
	DINNER			
	SNACKS			
	BEDTIME			

NOTES

_____

_____

_____

_____

SUNDAY		DATE:		
MEALS	**READINGS**	**BEFORE**	**AFTER**	**NOTES**
	BREAKFAST			
	LUNCH			
	DINNER			
	SNACKS			
	BEDTIME			

MONDAY		DATE:		
MEALS	**READINGS**	**BEFORE**	**AFTER**	**NOTES**
	BREAKFAST			
	LUNCH			
	DINNER			
	SNACKS			
	BEDTIME			

TUESDAY		DATE:		
MEALS	**READINGS**	**BEFORE**	**AFTER**	**NOTES**
	BREAKFAST			
	LUNCH			
	DINNER			
	SNACKS			
	BEDTIME			

WEDNESDAY		DATE:		
MEALS	**READINGS**	**BEFORE**	**AFTER**	**NOTES**
	BREAKFAST			
	LUNCH			
	DINNER			
	SNACKS			
	BEDTIME			

THURSDAY		DATE:		
MEALS	**READINGS**	**BEFORE**	**AFTER**	**NOTES**
	BREAKFAST			
	LUNCH			
	DINNER			
	SNACKS			
	BEDTIME			

FRIDAY		DATE:		
MEALS	**READINGS**	**BEFORE**	**AFTER**	**NOTES**
	BREAKFAST			
	LUNCH			
	DINNER			
	SNACKS			
	BEDTIME			

SATURDAY		DATE:		
MEALS	**READINGS**	**BEFORE**	**AFTER**	**NOTES**
	BREAKFAST			
	LUNCH			
	DINNER			
	SNACKS			
	BEDTIME			

NOTES

_____

_____

_____

_____

SUNDAY   DATE:

MEALS	READINGS	BEFORE	AFTER	NOTES
	BREAKFAST			
	LUNCH			
	DINNER			
	SNACKS			
	BEDTIME			

MONDAY   DATE:

MEALS	READINGS	BEFORE	AFTER	NOTES
	BREAKFAST			
	LUNCH			
	DINNER			
	SNACKS			
	BEDTIME			

TUESDAY   DATE:

MEALS	READINGS	BEFORE	AFTER	NOTES
	BREAKFAST			
	LUNCH			
	DINNER			
	SNACKS			
	BEDTIME			

WEDNESDAY   DATE:

MEALS	READINGS	BEFORE	AFTER	NOTES
	BREAKFAST			
	LUNCH			
	DINNER			
	SNACKS			
	BEDTIME			

THURSDAY		DATE:		
MEALS	**READINGS**	**BEFORE**	**AFTER**	**NOTES**
	BREAKFAST			
	LUNCH			
	DINNER			
	SNACKS			
	BEDTIME			

FRIDAY		DATE:		
MEALS	**READINGS**	**BEFORE**	**AFTER**	**NOTES**
	BREAKFAST			
	LUNCH			
	DINNER			
	SNACKS			
	BEDTIME			

SATURDAY		DATE:		
MEALS	**READINGS**	**BEFORE**	**AFTER**	**NOTES**
	BREAKFAST			
	LUNCH			
	DINNER			
	SNACKS			
	BEDTIME			

NOTES

_____

_____

_____

_____

Made in United States
North Haven, CT
02 January 2022

13979841R00063